EARLY CHILDHOOD
Religious Education
A to Z

EARLY CHILDHOOD

Religious Education

A to Z

Dr. Joseph D. White

Our Sunday Visitor
Huntington, Indiana

Nihil Obstat
Msgr. Michael Heintz, Ph.D.
Censor Librorum

Imprimatur
✠Kevin C. Rhoades
Bishop of Fort Wayne-South Bend

27 26 25 24 23 3 4 5 6 7 8 9

Our Sunday Visitor Publishing Division, Our Sunday Visitor, Inc., 200 Noll Plaza, Huntington, IN 46750; 1-800-348-2440; www.osv.com.

ISBN: 978-1-68192-640-7 (Inventory No. T2498)

Cover and interior design: Amanda Falk
Cover art: Shutterstock
Interior art: OSV photos; Shutterstock

PRINTED IN THE UNITED STATES OF AMERICA

Introduction

There aren't many things as rewarding as introducing young learners to God. This work sets the foundation for what we hope is a lifelong relationship with Jesus and his Church. You make an immeasurable difference to young children, whose brains are still growing in so many ways. This short booklet highlights key aspects of the art of faith formation with young children. Whether you are an early childhood catechist in a parish, a Catholic school prekindergarten or kindergarten teacher, a parent, a grandparent, or a godparent, if you want to help young learners discover their faith, this book is for you. Since kids this age are often learning their alphabet, I thought it fitting to present this with a point for each letter. From active learning to zany antics, prepare to reflect on twenty-six essential points about forming our youngest learners, and may God bless you in this important vocation!

A is for Active Learning

Young children think differently from older children and adults; they learn best by experiencing and doing. Abstract thought is still years away. Children between the ages of three and six need hands-on activities to do their best learning. A wealth of research in early childhood education has shown that workbook/worksheet-driven programs are not how young children learn best, and an academic approach to new material for children this age might even *hinder* learning (see, for example, "Play's Potential in Early Literacy Development," by James F. Christie & Kathleen A. Roskos, 2009; *The Hurried Child*, by David Elkin, 2001; etc.). As you plan your learning activities, be sure to include things children can see, hear, and touch. Arts and crafts, music, stories with pictures, dramatic play, and other activities that involve multiple senses are especially conducive to learning in early childhood. Include three-dimensional, hands-on materials. Build in lots of opportunities to move around the room.

B is for Bible Stories

As Catholics, we believe that God speaks to us through Sacred Scripture and Sacred Tradition. Children should know from an early age that the Bible is no ordinary book, since it contains the Word of God. Place a children's Bible in a prominent location in your learning area, and refer to it as you tell Bible stories. Use stories that are developmentally appropriate. Young children are not yet ready for some Scripture stories that may require more abstract thinking or include details that could be frightening for little ones. But our faith has been handed down as a story for many generations, from the time of our Jewish ancestors in faith. Many stories in Scripture are fun for young children to learn and help facilitate a beginning understanding of important principles of faith.

Use a curriculum that chooses stories from Scripture according to an intentional scope and sequence, identifying foundational principles of faith for young children and choosing Scripture stories that teach those principles. Use multisensory storytelling techniques, such as felt or magnetic figures. Children also love to act out stories they have learned. Simple Bible character costumes can be made from paper grocery bags or pieces of fabric in various lengths and colors.

C is for Crafts

Using arts and crafts activities in learning sessions with young children provides an active way to engage with the lesson material. However, be careful that craft activities aren't used simply as "fillers" for time. If you are using an early childhood curriculum that has a declaration of Conformity with the Catechism from the United States Conference of Catholic Bishops (which we highly recommend), each lesson will have a particular learning objective that is articulated in the catechist or teacher manual. The learning objective might be called the "main point" or "learning goal." It is usually only one or two lines long and will appear at the beginning of the chapter in your guide.

Choose a craft that can help to serve as a concrete visual reminder of that learning objective. For example, if the learning goal is, "Children will learn that the Holy Trinity is One God in Three Divine Persons," an appropriate craft activity would be to make a shamrock. Of course, you will want to talk with the children about how St. Patrick used the shamrock to teach others about God, since the shamrock has three leaves, but is one shamrock. Review what the craft project helps the children remember (the learning goal) by asking: "Why are we making these today? What do they help us to remember?" Because even a few months difference in age can make a difference in fine motor development, preschool and kindergarten children can vary in their motor skills. Be aware of this when choosing craft activities that involve cutting with scissors, lacing, or other advanced motor skills.

D is for Developmentally Appropriate

It's important that we always present lessons of faith in ways that are understandable and engaging for young children. Even if our content is theologically sound, if we don't make the material developmentally appropriate, they won't walk away with a proper understanding of the Faith. There are many facets to the development of young children.

Cognitive development refers to the way kids change in their understanding of concepts, the way they think about material, and it is often reflected in the language they use and the way in which their vocabulary grows.

Social development is a term we use to describe how young children grow and change in their ability to interact and get along with other people, including caregivers, teachers, and peers.

Emotional development refers to the way in which children understand and label their feelings and their ability to regulate their feelings, such as calming themselves when angry or upset.

Motor development is the way in which children grow in their coordination, balance, and ability to use big muscles (gross motor skills) and small muscles (fine motor skills).

Moral development refers to the way in which children grow in their understanding of rules and guidelines for behavior and how to make choices.

Spiritual development is the way children grow in their relationship with God.

As we plan activities, it's important to consider all these facets of development so we can meet children where they are.

E is for Empathy

Young kids need to know that we understand how they feel. It helps them feel safe and secure with us. Reflecting feelings is an important part of the work of both professionals and caregivers of young children. When we use a sympathetic tone to say things like, "I can see you are really frustrated about that," or "That makes you sad, doesn't it?" we help kids grow in three important ways. First, we help them learn to label their feelings. Developing *affective vocabulary*, or "feelings language," is an important first step toward regulation of emotions. We can't regulate (or control) what we can't identify. Also, when kids can tell we understand their feelings, it helps them to regulate them and calm down. We all feel a little better when we feel understood. Finally, when we model empathy by showing empathy to children, this helps children begin to develop empathy for others as well.

F is for Family

The *Catechism of the Catholic Church* tells us, "Parents receive the responsibility and privilege of *evangelizing their children*. Parents should initiate their children at an early age into the mysteries of the faith of which they are the 'first heralds' for their children" (2225). Parents are the first and most important teachers of the Faith for their children. It would be a disservice to the child and family for those of us who are catechists and religion teachers to take that responsibility away from parents. Rather, we are called to support families by making lessons of faith systematic and comprehensive, helping kids articulate what they should already be living in the home and parish with their families.

For this reason, we should make efforts to connect faith formation sessions with home and family life. One tool for doing this is to provide parents and families with "Ask Me" questions. These are one or two questions about the learning goal for each lesson that can be sent home with the parent so they can ask their child specific questions about what they learned. Include the answers as well, just in case the parent isn't sure! It's also helpful to send home a small action step a family could take over the course of the week to live the message of that week's lesson. In doing these two things, you will help parents grow in the ability to talk with their children about the Faith, and you might help parents grow in faith as well!

G is For Games

Kids love to play games. Games give us a chance to playfully reflect on lessons and try new things, and they help keep us engaged and excited. Games are an important part of the curriculum for early childhood learning. Children this age are learning how to share, take turns, and work together. They are also in an important stage of identity building where they are learning to feel more confident trying new things. For these reasons, it's best if we can use noncompetitive games if possible. It just takes a little creativity to make noncompetitive games just as exciting as competitive ones. For example, perhaps the kids are working as a team to solve a problem or complete a challenging task that none of them can do alone. Or perhaps they are one "team" working together to win against you, the group leader. (That will give you plenty of opportunities to ham it up and elicit some laughs, particularly if you are playfully annoyed when they score against you!)

Other games might merely involve playful, hands-on ways to talk about things in a group. When I am working with groups of young children, I like to play a game called "Feelings Ball," in which children sit in a circle and roll a ball back and forth across the circle. When one of the kids catches the ball, they will say a feeling they have today and why. They will then pass the ball across the circle to a friend. The game continues until everyone has had a chance to share. Feelings Ball is a great way to check in with everyone in the group at the beginning of your time together.

H is for Helpers

Because preschool and kindergarten children can be on so many different developmental levels within the same age group, they often will need help with something. However, it's best if you, as the catechist or teacher, don't take that responsibility all on yourself. Children can be taught at an early age to work together and help one another. Adopt the motto that, "As friends of Jesus, we help one another." In mixed-age groups, older learners can help younger ones. In same-age groups, identify talents and areas of need, and pair your learners in activities accordingly. It may be necessary to prompt kids to be helpful, as they might not yet have the social awareness to notice when someone needs help. Creating an atmosphere in which kids assist one another will foster confidence in kids who are helping and help to build a community that is inclusive and responsive to others, which is what the Church, as the Body of Christ, is called to be.

I is for Independence

As you plan learning activities, consider whether your activities are *teacher/catechist-directed* or *child-directed*. Child-directed activities (activities children can complete independently) have been shown to be most effective in learning new content in early childhood and maintaining a positive attitude toward learning. Preschool and kindergarten children learn best when they can guide themselves through activities. It can be helpful to prepare materials and lay them out before your learning session so kids can move from area to area enjoying the activities you have prepared. You might wish to have a class meeting in the form of "circle time" at the beginning of your session, where you will explain each of the activity options and even demonstrate how to do them. As the children explore the activities you have set up for them around the room, circulate so you can praise them on their work and be a resource if they need help.

J is for Jesus

In his apostolic exhoration *Catechesi Tradendae* (On Catechesis in Our Time), Pope Saint John Paul II wrote, "the definitive aim of catechesis is to put people not only in touch but in communion, in intimacy, with Jesus Christ" (5). For Christians, everything in our faith revolves around the central axis of Jesus. Therefore, it makes sense to introduce Jesus first.

If young children get to know Jesus, everything they learn after that will be in its proper context. For example, we can't understand the Blessed Virgin Mary and her role in our faith unless we understand her relationship to Jesus. Children should understand Jesus as God and king, but also as friend and brother. These various aspects of our understanding of Jesus can be conveyed through stories such as the triumphant entry into Jerusalem, Jesus' welcome of little children, Jesus' miracles, and his visit as a twelve-year-old child to the Temple. While we must never lose sight of the divinity of Jesus, and need to make this clear to our learners, it is his humanity and his gentle approachability that will draw young children to him, as was the case in his ministry on earth.

K is For Kindness

Preschool and kindergarten children are naturally egocentric — many of them believe the world revolves around them and that others see the world just the way they do. This isn't a character flaw, it's just a normal stage in their understanding of themselves and others. Still, a primary task of these early years is to grow in social skills, particularly in *pro-social behavior*, which we might describe as positive, kind behaviors toward others. Some of the most important lessons learned during the early childhood years are in the area of social development, including sharing, taking turns, making friends, respecting others' feelings and space, and social problem-solving. Many young children will need some prompting and coaching in order to learn to do these things naturally and effectively. Sit with your learners as they interact with one another. Coach children through challenging interactions, reflecting the feelings of all the children in the situation. Offer suggestions, and role model appropriate responses. In this way, you are helping children learn how to fulfill Jesus' commandment: "As I have loved you, so you also should love one another" (Jn 13:34).

L is for Liturgy

The Catholic Church worships and celebrates together. An essential part of forming young children to know and love the Church is helping them to understand our Church calendar and how we celebrate together. A "classroom altar" or prayer space in the room where catechetical sessions are held can be helpful in teaching about the liturgy. Use a simple end table or decorator table, and cover it with a white tablecloth. Buy cloth napkins in the colors used in the liturgical year (green, violet, gold, and red). Use the appropriate color for the season as an accent on the top of the classroom altar. Then place sacred objects such as a crucifix, rosary, icons, or statues. You might also wish to place flowers and a battery-operated candle in the sacred space. When the colors of the Church year change, make a big production of changing the color and objects on the classroom altar, and talk about why. A children's Mass kit can be a helpful way to talk about the vessels used in the liturgy in a hands-on, multisensory way. Finally, if possible, go on a "field trip" to the Church. Talk about the many things children can see in the Church and what they mean.

M is for Music and Movement

Music is helpful in early childhood classrooms for a variety of reasons. Most young children enjoy music, and when paired with movement, such as hand gestures, singing together becomes a multisensory activity. Active movement set to music helps little ones get extra wiggles out so they are ready for times when they need to be more still. In general, our attention span is equal to our age in minutes until the early twenties, due to the continued growth of the prefrontal cortex (the attention center of the brain) during these years. Knowing that attention span is equal to age in minutes can strike fear in the hearts of early childhood teachers and catechists. (That means we only have their attention for three to six minutes!) But movement helps to reset the "attention clock" in the brain. It's why we shift positions when we are sitting and listening to a long lecture, and why kids move around even more. Also, music helps us remember concepts better. Pairing words to be learned with music and rhythm can make memorizing concepts as simple as learning a song. If possible, use music that is written for preschool and kindergarten children, and select songs that reinforce the learning objectives of the lesson.

N is For Nature

Young children are naturally curious, and they love to explore and learn about God's creation. Take the group outside when possible. Perhaps you can go on a prayer walk around the parish or school grounds. Ask kids to notice and name things in nature that they see as you are walking together, and pause to say a prayer of thanksgiving for each aspect of creation they notice. When the weather does not permit exploration outside, bring nature into the classroom. For example, you might wish to bring fall leaves to assist in a discussion about the seasons or for use in a craft project. On a rainy day in the spring, you might talk about how God sends rain to help plants and flowers grow. Perhaps you could plant some seeds in small jars and open the window, catching some rainwater in each jar. Finally, incorporate books that help children learn about various aspects of creation. Place these in your reading center, and talk about them when the lesson is on the Creation story or the changing of the seasons.

O is for Organization

The field of environmental psychology is built on research showing that our environment changes the way we feel and behave. Disorganization can sap our energy, and we need plenty of energy when we are working with young children. For children, a well-organized space can lead to better self-regulation and behavior. Any space used for faith formation should be interesting, but not cluttered. Is there enough in the room to say, "Exciting things happen here"? Is the room organized and clean? If possible, arrange the room in advance in a way that makes sense for the activities you have planned. A good general arrangement for children's catechesis should include an area for table activities and a gathering space for circle time. Be sure to put away anything you don't want the children to get into, and have your activity supplies prepared and ready. A little extra time invested before the session can save an hour of frustration and stress.

P is for Prayer

An essential part of forming kids in faith is teaching them how to talk with God. The expressions of prayer we utilize with children should depend in part on their age and developmental level. Young children will benefit a great deal from the use of pictures and statues. They may be encouraged to say "Hi" or "I love you" to Jesus depicted in a statue or painting. They can be taught to make the Sign of the Cross and can be taught prayers set to music. As children get older, they should be taught both spontaneous and traditional Catholic prayers. Traditional prayers are valuable because they enable us to pray together, in unison, as God's people. They also give us a repertoire from which to choose when we are not sure what to pray; but they should be introduced gradually as children are able to understand them. It's important that children learn about all the different *forms* of prayer, as articulated in the *Catechism* (see 2626–43).

It can be helpful to choose a form of prayer to pray each week when gathered around the classroom altar. For example, you might say: "Today, we are going to pray thank-you prayers. Let's go around the circle and each name one thing we want to thank God for. After each person says what they would like to thank God for, we'll all say together, 'Thank you, God.'" On another day, we might do something similar with prayers of intercession, saying: "Today, let's think of a person who needs God's help. We'll go around the circle, and each of us can pray for a person who needs God's help. After each person prays, he or she can say, 'We pray to the Lord,' and we will all respond, 'Lord, hear our prayer.'" Note how this way of praying follows the rhythm of the prayers of the faithful in Mass. This will prepare your learners to actively participate in this portion of the liturgy.

Q is for Quiet Time

We live in a noisy, fast-paced world. Experts in child development are understandably concerned about the impact of this hectic environment on the young child's developing brain. The use of silence and voice modulation can be calming to young children, can help to pace the lesson, and can impart a sense of reverence. When the group is noisy and you need them to prepare for a quieter activity, such as prayer time, resist the urge to talk loudly over the children. Instead, in a quiet voice, say, "If you can hear my voice, raise your hand." Only the children nearest to you will raise their hands, but this will get the other children's attention. Repeat the sentence again. This time more children will raise their hands as the room quiets. Repeat the sentence once more. Eventually, everyone will be quieter and ready to hear what you say next.

When telling stories, change your pace, and use pauses of silence in strategic places so children will engage with the story more and anticipate what might happen next. In prayer times and other times of reverence, invite children to become quiet with you and pause for a brief moment. Over time, you can extend this moment of silence a bit as children are ready.

R is for Relationship

Advances in neuroscience and child development have helped us better understand that two of the primary tasks of young children are forming attachments and learning how to grow in relationship with others, and this corresponds with rapid growth in the relational areas of the brain. A preschool program that introduces children to Jesus as both God and friend and introduces the parish church or Catholic school as a community of friends, an extended family, will assist the child in developing an attachment to the Faith at exactly the time that the attachment mechanisms in the brain are growing most rapidly. This attachment then sets the context for a systematic presentation of the basic teachings of the Faith during the school year.

With an already-existing relationship of attachment to Jesus and the Church, the fundamentals of the Faith take on a new significance. Children who are aware of and growing in their relationship with Christ do not view religion classes in the parish or school simply as another academic exercise. They *want* to learn more about the one they *love*.

S is for Saints

We have a shortage of good role models in popular culture today, so it's more important than ever to point children to our heroes in faith — the Communion of Saints. Share stories of our Catholic saints often, taking care to ensure that you choose saints whose stories are not too intense for young learners — for example, stories of martyrs or saints that died as children might be too disturbing at this age. Be sure to include stories of both male and female saints, as well as saints of various racial and ethnic backgrounds. We want children to see themselves in the saints so they know that it is possible for them to live holy lives as well. In addition to sharing stories of saints, bring icons or statues of saints to share. It might also be fun for the children to dress up as saints and to act out some saint stories. If you have a dramatic-play center in your classroom, include costumes that represent various saints. Show the costumes along with pictures of the saints, and talk about ways children can pretend to be that saint. For example, you might show a picture of Saint Francis near his feast day and talk about how he loved to show God's love to animals. Then, place a brown robe in the dramatic play area along with several stuffed animals.

T is for Tasty Treats

Much of Jesus' ministry was centered around a meal — from his first miracle at a wedding feast, to his meals with tax collectors and sinners, to his Last Supper with his disciples before his death, to the meals by the seashore and on the road to Emmaus after his resurrection. And this is no accident. Social science researchers have found that we communicate better with and draw closer to those with whom we share food. Eating together helps us to form and maintain community. That's one reason why snack time can be so important to a group of early childhood learners. Another reason is that the fast metabolism of young children leads them to get hungry more often, and it can be hard to learn when you're hungry!

Kids love to make their own snacks. Easy to assemble snacks that are connected to the lesson can be a fun, multisensory, and tasty way to learn. Be conscious of food allergies. Be sure to get this information from parents at the beginning of the year, and let parents know in advance what you will be serving.

U is For Us

When it comes to making moral decisions, preschool children are in the process of moving from *preconventional moral reasoning*, when choices are made based on rewards or punishments, praise or disapproval, to *conventional moral reasoning*, when children begin to choose actions based on the rules or norms for groups or communities of which they are members. In other words, they go from simply seeking positive consequences and avoiding negative ones to feeling a sense of community identity and behaving in ways that are acceptable within the group. For this reason, we want to help foster a healthy sense of Catholic identity and an identification with their Catholic community of peers. As you introduce rules and guidelines for behavior, talk about how those rules are connected with loving God and loving others. Clearly state the rule in connection with our identity as followers of Jesus. For example, you might say, "As friends of Jesus, we share and take turns with one another."

V is for Virtues

Although they are still growing in self-control and learning to follow rules, young children usually are not so set in their ways that they have already gotten into firmly ingrained bad habits of behavior. This gives us a perfect opportunity to start them off right, to get into good habits of behavior before the bad ones are learned. As good habits get established, they become virtues — spiritual habits that strengthen and enable us to do what is right and good. We received the three theological virtues — faith, hope and charity — at baptism, so it's our job to nourish the soil that these seeds have been planted in, helping children grow in and express these three virtues. The cardinal virtues (prudence, justice, fortitude, and temperance) will take time and grace to develop as children mature. However, we can lay the foundation for these virtues as we coach kids to "stop and think" before they act, help them understand the difference between right and wrong, offer encouragement to keep trying when something is challenging, and establish clear limits for their behavior.

W is for Witness

The Church teaches that everyone who is baptized is a missionary, including our youngest learners! We are all called to share the good news of Jesus in both word and action. You can help children share what they have learned in a number of ways. First, talk about the learning objective, or the main point of the lesson, throughout your session. Connect everything you do back to that main point — for example, "We are looking at this story today, because we are learning [main point]," or "We are singing this song, because it's a song about [main point]." After you have repeated the main point several times throughout the learning activities, at the end of your time together, ask the kids to tell you what they learned. See if they can repeat the main point to you. If you have made a craft project, ask them what the project reminds us of. (They will hopefully reply with the main point!)

Talk about, and practice, ways to live out the faith lessons being learned. For example, if you are talking about loving others, role-play some ways to show love by helping others. Kids love to pretend, and we are more likely to do the things we practice.

X is for X-tra Planning

One of the things that keeps work with young children interesting is that you can't always tell what might happen. Some activities go longer than expected. Others are over in no time at all. We might find that something we planned just doesn't fit with the developmental level of our learners. Or, on some days, schedules might change, and you'll need to extend an activity. For all of these reasons, it's important to do a little extra planning. Have an activity ready for children to get started with right away as they arrive. That way, kids who arrive early aren't waiting around for something to happen, or worse yet finding something to do that might get them into trouble. Having an activity on the table that children can do independently as they arrive also offers you the opportunity to have quick conversations with parents, which will strengthen your role as a support to moms and dads, who are the primary faith teachers of their children. Be sure to have some extra activities handy in case they are needed for the reasons described above. If you don't get to them, you can always save them for another day.

Y is For You

The *General Directory for Catechesis*, one of the foundational documents that has guided faith formation in the last few decades, says this: "No methodology, no matter how well tested, can dispense with the person of the catechist in every phase of the catechetical process" (156). That is to say, when it comes to forming kids in faith, *you* are more important than the materials you use and the activities you plan. Your witness, your example, is your most important tool for teaching what it means to be a disciple of Jesus. You are the face of the Church for many young children who are coming to the parish or school community for the first time (or at least for the first time in an environment designed especially for them). Your patience, warmth, and kindness will speak volumes about who we are as Catholics.

Z is for Zany

When we work with young children, it's important not to take ourselves too seriously. Let your hair down, and be a little silly. It will make you seem more approachable, and will help the kids feel more comfortable. Kids love slapstick. Being a little clumsy on purpose is guaranteed to get some laughs from kids. Pretending not to know things kids know will offer them a chance to share what they have learned and lead to some good laughs also. Having a laugh together helps kids realize that the Christian community is a joyful place.